Creation of Photobook for Beginners

Making of Photo book Manually and Automatically

Richard A.E

All rights reserved. No part of this publication may be reproduced, distributed, or transmitted in any form or by any means, including photocopying, recording, or other electronic or mechanical methods, without the prior written permission of the publisher, except in the case of brief quotations embodied in critical reviews and certain other noncommercial uses permitted by copyright law.

Copyright © (Richard A.E), (20203).

Table of Content

Chapter 1
Chapter 2
Chapter 3

Chapter 1

Describe a photo book

The photo book is a collection of images by a photographer that has a unifying subject or follows a narrative. It is a practical and fairly priced approach to introduce photography to a wide audience.

PHOTOBOOK
The photo book is a collection of images by a photographer that has a unifying subject or follows a narrative. It is a practical and fairly priced approach to introduce photography to a wide audience.

Early photobooks served as examples of a photographer's particular work or a novel photography technique. In 1844, William Henry Fox Talbot released a photobook titled The Pencil of Nature to publicize his calotype photographing technique.

Photobooks have contributed to the concept that a picture sequence may serve as a standalone story over time. The face of Our Time, part of the lifelong endeavor of the German photographer August Sander to compile a thorough photographic registry of the German people, was released in 1929.

Photobooks are now essential for funding and disseminating contemporary photography, giving fans access to a variety of artists from throughout the globe.

Sizes of photo books: 5×14, 8×16, 20×24, 10×20, 12×16, 18×24.

so on.

Chapter 2

Materials required to create a photo book

The backbone of the photo book is a strawboard.

*Utility knife - Used to cut paper, PVC, and foam boards, among other materials.

*Ruler - Measurements are done using a ruler

*Elbow stick glue - is used to adhere the paper to the back cover.

*Thread.

*Oil for Coating.

*PVC or a sketchbook.

*Kerosine- If a restart or clean-up of the job is required, this reduces the impact of the glue.

Equipment required to create a photo book

Coating Machine:

UV coating is a great method to stand out in print marketing materials, according to the coating machine: Your business cards, postcards, flyers, and other items will have a stunning glossy finish thanks to UV coating. The most value for your marketing buck comes from having your print marketing materials UV coated, which adds a thick layer of protection for enduring durability. What exactly is UV coating, how does it function, and what are the advantages and benefits for your print job? The following explains UV treatment and why print marketing materials need it.

Describe UV coating.

When a transparent substance called UV coating is put to damp paper, ultraviolet light quickly dries it (UV coating is short for ultraviolet coating). Paper is coated with a variety of substances; chemicals used for UV coating include polyethylene, calcium carbonate, and kaolinite. These substances are purified and combined with viscosifiers, which aid in their ability to stick to the paper. After printing, the coating is applied using a UV coating equipment.

Depending on the purpose, UV coatings may range in thickness and reflectivity, while high-gloss or soft matte UV coatings are often employed for high-end printing applications.

Your product might have a UV coating on every surface, simply one side, or the front and rear. You may also choose spot UV coating, which applies an ultraviolet layer selectively to certain areas of your design (a great way to make logos or photos stand out).

Is a UV coating water-resistant? UV coating is water resistant but not waterproof.

It is important to distinguish between UV coating and other paper finishing techniques like aqueous coating and lamination.

Aqueous coating vs. UV coating: While UV coating provides more gloss and better protection, aqueous coating is water-based and might be an excellent coating choice for paper.

Lamination gives decent protection, however, the lamination process necessitates edge-cutting, which might raise manufacturing costs. UV coating offers better protection. While UV coating does not give waterproofing, lamination may

As you can see, the UV coating method is unique from conventional paper treatments and has a number of distinct benefits.

Binding Machine:

A binding machine is used to bind a variety of papers, including manuals, quotes, brochures, and many other types of materials. Instead of paying to have the job outsourced to another company, using a binder helps manage in-house printing for a business. Purchasing a binding machine in Malaysia can make the printed materials you create for your consumers and clients seem more polished. It should be your preferred technique for presenting any significant documents.

There are numerous varieties of binding machines accessible in the market according to their usage, such as manual binding machines and electric binding machines in Malaysia, depending on specific demands in the workplace or industry. Since they all follow a relatively similar procedure, they come in all different sizes and forms. The comb, wire, and coil binding forms are the three most often used types. VeloBind is popular with users who want to produce crisp papers. Each of these styles for binding is intended to bind many pieces of paper together.

Most binding machines work in only 4 simple steps:

1. You must first set up the machine, which often entails changing the side margin control to make sure the holes are being punched where they should be. To check that everything is set up and working correctly, you must first punch one sheet of paper. Make more modifications if the holes are incorrect.

2. You may start punching holes in the paper you want to bind once you set up the machine. A machine's capacity, which varies from machine to machine, will determine how much paper it can bind.

3. Following the completion of all the holes, you may start putting the binding element into the openings. You will then need to finish the book. This entails shutting the wire or the comb in the case of combs. However, with the coil, this entails trimming the extra coil and wrapping the ends.

As you can see, binding is a really simple operation. Contact EasiTech, which has ten years of expertise with binding machines, if you're looking for any kind of binding machine. They provide an enormous selection of binding devices, including Bindomatic binding devices, plastic comb binding devices, spiral binding devices, book binding devices, and many more.

Chapter 3

Manually

The exterior

Starting with the Cover Page this will appear on the front page of the photobook or design, starting with the front page.

Step 1:
Measure the straw board to the size you want your photo book or cover page to be before beginning your cover page. Measure the photo book, the straw board, or the cover page in inches. Measure the front and back of the photobook separately before cutting it out with a utility knife. The cover page should be long and wide enough to cover the front and back of the photo book and fold.

Step 2:
After applying your elbow stick gum, wait for four to five minutes before removing it from the cover page and straw board. Place a straw board in the center of the cover page and the front and back pages of the picture

book. After you've placed the straw board on the cover page, fold the sides and edges inwards.

Interior Section

Step 1:
After printing the photo for the photo book, organize the photos by number, cost the page, and then divide or fold it into two equal half.

Step 2:
Next, bond the book using PVC or a sketchpad. Using PVC, take the picture and paste it to one side of the PVC after removing the nylon on it. Then, arrange the pictures according to their numbers. Repeat this process with the remaining pictures until you've added all the PVC with the pictures you need or want to use. Place the first page of a piece of cardboard or paper on the PVC's final face. Then you put them in numerical order and use elbow stick glue to adhere the pictures to the P.V.C. in a manner that allows you to open and close it like a book. Not too much adhesive should be used, and As soon as all of the pictures are in book shape, start at the top of the back side and work your way down.

When using a sketch pad, you'll utilize elbow stick glue more. To use it, collect your pictures and sketch pads first, then paste the glue on the sketch pad's face and the picture's back to adhere the two together. Continue doing this, then finish by placing the front page or cardstock paper on the last page of the sketchbook. Then put them in a book form and glue the back of the book until it takes on the shape of a book, arranging them in accordance with the order you assigned the photographs.

Note:Be sure the image isn't erupting from the top or side of the sketchpad or P.V.C.

Step 3:
Measure and cut the book after binding.

In other words, you cut the Book to the desired size. using the Binding Machine's Cutting Machine fiction. Then close the straw board after placing your book on it, leaving it to dry for a day or 16–18 hours.

Automatically:

HOW TO MAKE A DIGITAL PHOTO BOOK: MY STEP-BY-STEP PROCESS

1. Upload pictures from your event into an album using Photos for Mac.
Have questions about creating a digital picture book? Choose your event's top pictures (s)

If you finished the Digital Photo Organizing Challenge, you are aware that I save all of my digital images in one location on the hard drive of my computer and use a standard file structure to keep them organized. However, when it comes to making a picture book, I believe that photo organizing software may be very useful.

I use Photos for Mac since I use a Mac (the native photo organizing software that comes built into newer Mac computers, replacing iPhoto in recent years). I start by importing all of the photos from a particular event into Photos, where I then transfer the photos into an album I make for the occasion.

The next stage in the procedure is to narrow down that number and choose Pictures.

2. Use the Favorites feature to filter photographs.

Have questions about creating a digital picture book? Choose Favorites, then make a new album under Photos to save them.

You may easily browse through your photos (individually or collectively) in the Photos app and choose a subset of them using the Favorites feature. Simply click on the heart in the top-left corner of the picture to mark it as a favorite; a solid white heart means that you've already done so.

3. Make a new album with just the photos you like.
Have questions about creating a digital picture book? Using a picture management tool like Photos, choose between 80 and 100 images.

After I've narrowed down my picture collection, I make a separate album with only the photos I've marked as Favorites to include into the photo book. I gave the second album in this effort the moniker Favorite Photo Book.

Edit the photos you've chosen for your digital picture book using Photos.
Have questions about creating a digital picture book? EDIT your photographs PRIOR to importing them into a photo book program.

I make any necessary adjustments to each picture in this new folder using the Photos App. The picture is usually sharpened, brightened, and the white balance is changed throughout my editing process.

Depending on the project, you may have to do more or less editing at this stage. The lighting in the natatorium where he swam wasn't great, so I had to manually adjust practically every photo.

Despite the fact that the majority of photo book software packages have editing features built into their platforms, I believe that the editing possibilities are fairly limited and difficult to use.

Before uploading your photographs to the photo book website, I strongly advise retouching them with a photo editing application. In this manner, you'll be able to modify the photographs much more rapidly and with more control.

5. Export modified photos into a new desktop folder.
Have questions about creating a digital picture book? Publish edited photos from Photos

Once you've finished editing your photos, export them from the Photos app and place them in a new folder on your computer's hard drive (I like to create a new folder on my computer desktop, but you can save this folder anywhere that makes sense to you).

Make sure the photos ARE NOT exported as "UNMODIFIED ORIGINALS." If you do, all of the edits you made throughout the editing process will have been lost.

You now have a single folder on your computer with a collection of altered pictures that you've decided to include in your photo book. Yey!

From this point on, I'll demonstrate how to make a picture book using Mixbook, a digital photo book service. You can use a lot of other sites to make a beautiful digital picture book, but none of them are as simple to use as Mixbook.

Create a new project in Mixbook and choose a book design.
Have questions about creating a digital picture book? Choose a simple picture book provider like Mixbook to get started.

I selected the option to make a picture book once I was in Mixbook.

I then decided on a design concept, a book size, and a book shape. I made a landscape-oriented 11 x 8.5-inch album for my MegaZones collection:

Have questions about creating a digital picture book? Choose an album size and layout theme first.

There are a ton of different design theme options on Mixbook. I am drawn to designs in the minimalist portfolio style. You may use as many accessories as you like if you want a typical scrapbook layout!

7. Upload pictures to Mixbook

Have questions about creating a digital picture book? From your PC or a photo-storage website, upload your images.

Uploading your photographs to Mixbook is quite easy. Do you still have in mind the folder you made when you exported your photos from the Photos app? Simply click the "Upload Photos" button after navigating to that folder.

Afterward, you'll observe your photos being uploaded one by one:

Have questions about creating a digital picture book? Initially, enter images into the design program.

8. Start your design!
When all of your photos have been submitted, here is when things really start to heat up!

I prefer to start my album cover design process from scratch (which is always the meet logo for these championship swim meet albums).

Have questions about creating a digital picture book? Simply add your images and start creating your pages.

There is a pre-formatted layout for each page that comes with the theme I picked for this book (Bold White), but I seldom ever use it. Instead, I like to build each page specifically depending on the quantity of photographs I want to utilize. I can easily make these unique layout adjustments using Mixbook.

I choose which photographs to put on a page and the layout I want to use for those particular images by switching between the "Photos" and "Layouts" tabs in the top left corner of the screen as I go through the design process. After that, inserting the photographs into the layout design is as simple as dragging and dropping them there:

Have questions about creating a digital picture book? Start with a simple page layout.

Text is very simple to include on a page. Simply click the "Add Text" button, choose your font's color, size, and style, and start typing:

Have questions about creating a digital picture book? Utilize Mixbook's simple drag & drop feature.

See those green checkmarks in the collection of thumbnail pictures up top? So that you don't have to keep track, they say that you contributed those photographs to the book. another nice Mixbook feature.

Have questions about creating a digital picture book? Use the Mixbook program to design a unique cover and spine.

Don't forget to give your picture book a title on the spine!

9. Create a preview of your picture book and carefully go over everything.

Almost all websites that provide picture book services provide you the option to create a preview of your photo book so that you may carefully evaluate it before making a purchase. Before letting you buy anything, they'll often ask you to click a box indicating that you have checked it for faults.

Phot Book types

*Hardcover. Sturdy, glossy cover; perfect bound with semi-gloss pages.

*Layflat Hardcover. Sturdy, glossy cover; thick layflat pages; satin finish.

Premium Layflat Hardcover. ...
Softcover.
Matte Cover.
Glossy Pages.
Linen Books.
Leather Books.

Use of a Photo book

*Skills acquisition.
*Photo books provide a fun way to organize all the photos you've taken. They are also an impressive way to relive memories with your friends and family. However you choose to make your photo books, make sure to add unique touches to make it extra personal.

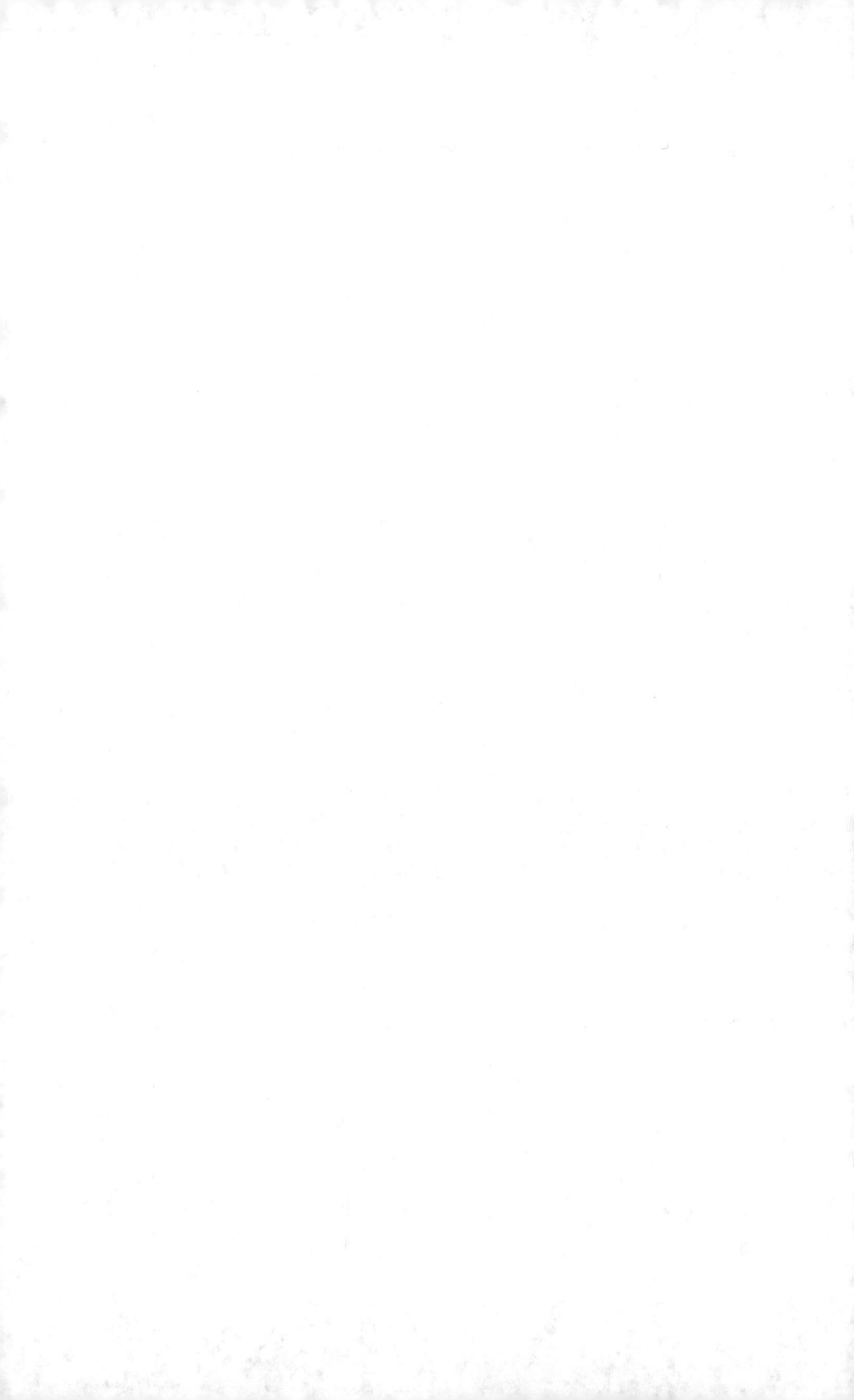

www.ingramcontent.com/pod-product-compliance
Lightning Source LLC
Chambersburg PA
CBHW070322220526
45465CB00013B/2195